Would You RULES

- MORE PLAYERS MEANS MORE FUN (MINIMUM 2 PLAYERS)

- LOTS OF PEOPLE? PLAY IN TEAMS - BUT YOU MUST ALL AGREE ON AN ANSWER WITH A REASON!

- CHOOSE A PLAYER TO GO FIRST
  ANOTHER PLAYER ASKS THEM A QUESTION

- EACH PERSON HAS TO DECIDE THEIR ANSWER
  YOU CAN MAKE A RULE THAT THEY HAVE TO EXPLAIN THE ANSWER

- THE GAME IS FLEXIBLE - PLAY WITH THE RULES YOU WANT

- TEACHERS OR A PARTY OF KIDS CAN PLAY BY A SHOW OF HANDS OR MOVING TO A SPECIFIC PART OF THE ROOM TO INDICATE THEIR ANSWER.

- ABOVE ALL - HAVE FUN!
  LOTS OF SPOOKY FUN!

© Alex Smart 2020 All Rights Reserved

Would You Rather....

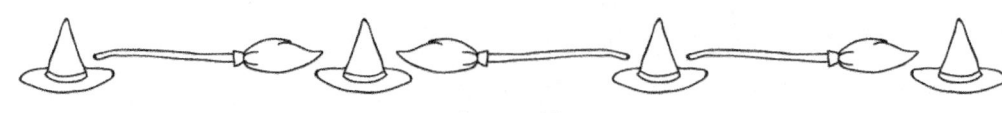

Touch a creepy crawly spider

OR

Stroke a slippery snake?

Would You Rather....

Spend the night in a haunted house ghost hunting

OR

Be a ghost who haunts a haunted house?

Would You Rather....

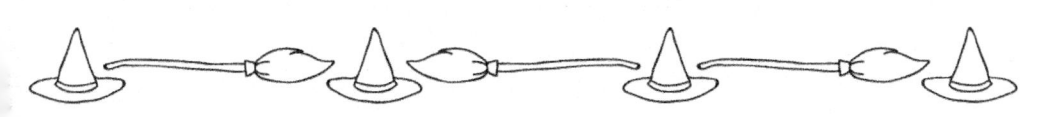

Hear a bloodcurdling screaM **OR** Feel a ghostly hand touch you?

Would You Rather....

Be bitten by a Vampire

OR

Be bitten by a Zombie?

WOULD YOU RATHER....

Be invited to a halloween party

OR

Enjoy trick or treat fun?

WOULD YOU RATHER....

PLAY A TRICK ON SOMEONE

OR

GIVE SOMEONE A LOVELY TREAT?

WOULD YOU RATHER....

CARVE A PUMPKIN

OR

DECORATE THE HOUSE FOR HALLOWEEN?

WOULD YOU RATHER....

MEET A ZOMBIE OR MEET A GHOST?

Would You Rather....

Wear a devil costume

OR

Wear a skeleton costume?

WOULD YOU RATHER...

HAVE A PET BAT

OR

HAVE A PET CAT?

Would You Rather....

Cast an evil spell

OR

Place a curse on someone?

WOULD YOU RATHER...

HAVE A FRIEND WHO IS A WIZARD

OR

HAVE A FRIEND WHO IS A WITCH?

WOULD YOU RATHER....

Stroke a tarantula
or
Stroke a snake?

WOULD YOU RATHER....

HAVE SUPERNATURAL POWERS

OR

BE SPINE TINGLING SCARY?

WOULD YOU RATHER.....

Hide in a dark shadow
or
Hide behind a tombstone?

WOULD YOU RATHER....

OWN A PET OWL

OR

OWN A MAGIC WAND?

Would You Rather....

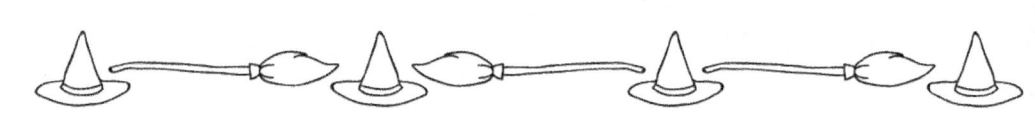

Spend the night in a haunted house **OR** Spend the night in a graveyard?

Would You Rather....

Be surrounded by fog **OR** Be surrounded by darkness?

Would You Rather....

Hold an eyeball

OR

Hold a slimy snail?

Would You Rather....

Eat as much candy as you wish but then the remainder is taken away

OR

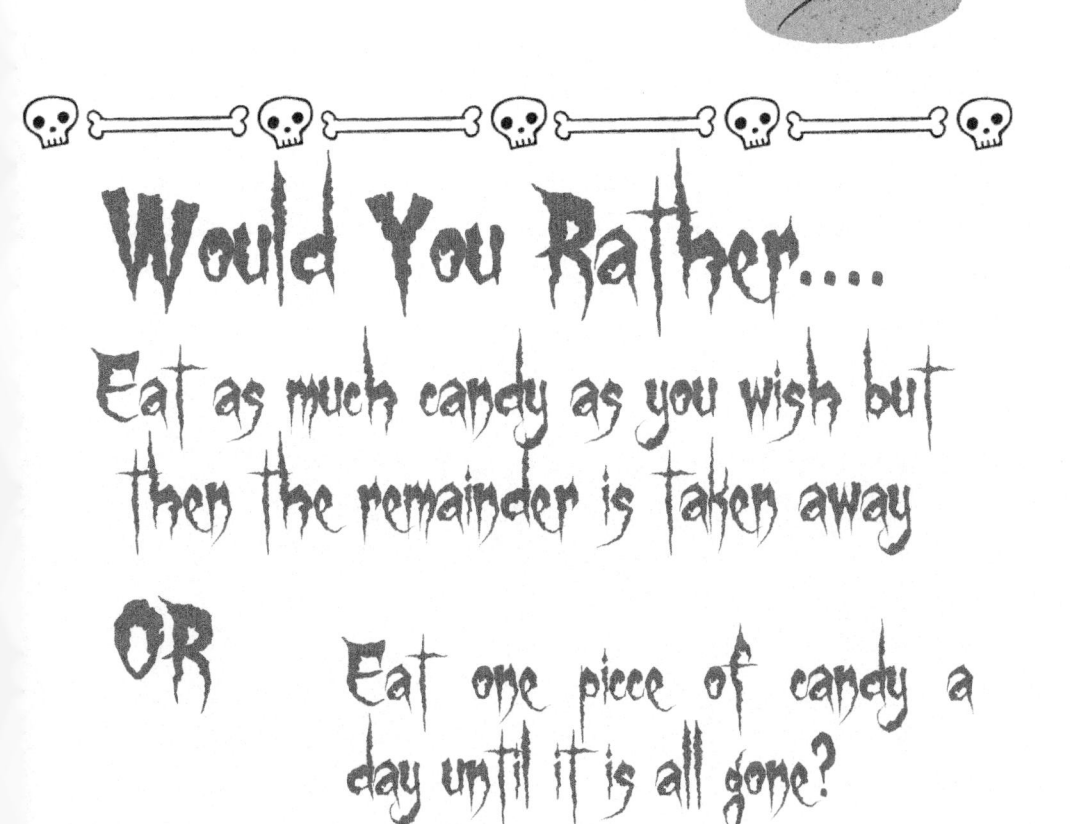

Eat one piece of candy a day until it is all gone?

WOULD YOU RATHER....

BECOME A VAMPIRE

OR

BECOME A WAREWOLF?

WOULD YOU RATHER....

READ A SPOOKY STORY **OR** WATCH A SPOOKY MOVIE?

WOULD YOU RATHER....

GO TRICK OR TREATING WITH FRIENDS

OR

GET PAID TO TAKE A LITTLE KID TRICK OR TREATING?

WOULD YOU RATHER....

SLEEP IN A COFFIN **OR** SLEEP IN A MONSTER'S CAVE?

Would You Rather....

Have a hand from the ground try to grab you?

OR

Be chased by a zombie

WOULD YOU RATHER...

OWN A SKULL

OR

OWN A VAMPIRE'S CAPE?

Would You Rather....

Wear only black clothes

OR

Wear only orange clothes?

WOULD YOU RATHER...

WALK LIKE A ZOMBIE

OR

PROWL LIKE A CAT?

WOULD YOU RATHER....

Be a good witch
or
Be a bad witch?

WOULD YOU RATHER....

BE WRAPPED UP LIKE A MUMMY

OR

HAVE BIG CLOWN FEET?

WOULD YOU RATHER....

Walk through cobwebs
or
Drink a witch's potion?

WOULD YOU RATHER....

CARRY A PUMPKIN AROUND ALL DAY

OR

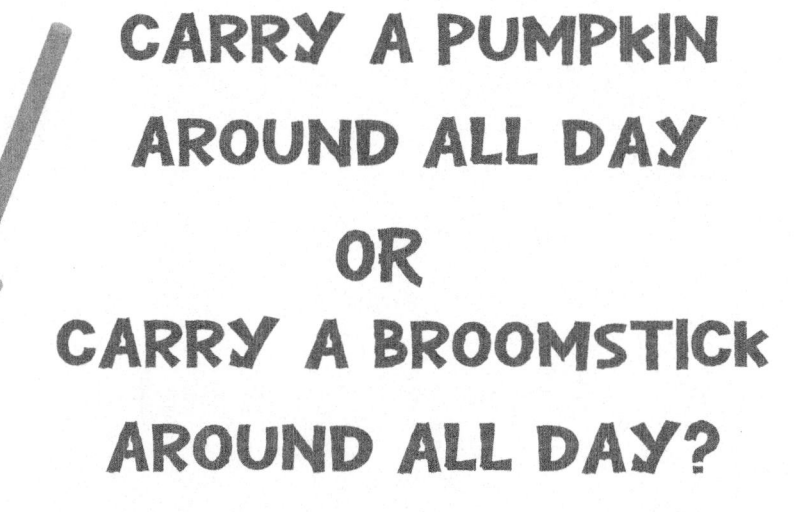

CARRY A BROOMSTICK AROUND ALL DAY?

Would You Rather....

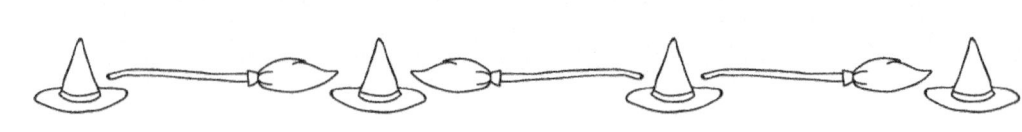

Live in a haunted house? **OR** Live in a creepy old castle?

Would You Rather....

Look after a black cat

OR

Look after a snowy white owl

Would You Rather....

Eat MUMMY cupcakes

OR

Eat skeleton cookies?

Would You Rather....

Jump in a pile of leaves

OR

Swing on a creeky swing?

WOULD YOU RATHER....

WEAR A SCARY COSTUME

OR

WEAR A CUTE COSTUME?

WOULD YOU RATHER....

TELL A GHOST STORY IN THE DARK

OR

LISTEN TO A GHOST STORY IN THE DARK?

WOULD YOU RATHER....

Be out on a dark and stormy night

OR

Be out on a cold but calm night?

WOULD YOU RATHER....

EAT AN APPLE DONUT **OR** EAT A CHOCOLATE CUPCAKE?

Would You Rather....

Find a knife with blood on

OR

Find a severed finger?

WOULD YOU RATHER...

HOOT LIKE AN OWL
OR
PURRR LIKE A CAT?

Would You Rather....

scoop out a large pumpkin with your bare hands

OR

Poke your finger into an eyeball?

WOULD YOU RATHER...

FIND A GHOST IN YOUR BATHROOM

OR

FIND A SCARY CLOWN IN YOUR BATHROOM?

WOULD YOU RATHER.....

Wear a costume with fake teeth

or

Wear a costume with an itchy wig?

WOULD YOU RATHER....

EAT 10 RAW PUMPKIN SEEDS

OR

EAT 10 RAW APPLE PIPS?

WOULD YOU RATHER.....

Jump out and scare a friend
or
Jump out and scare your teacher?

WOULD YOU RATHER....

SIT IN A TUB OF BLOOD

OR

SIT IN A TUB OF PUMPKIN SOUP?

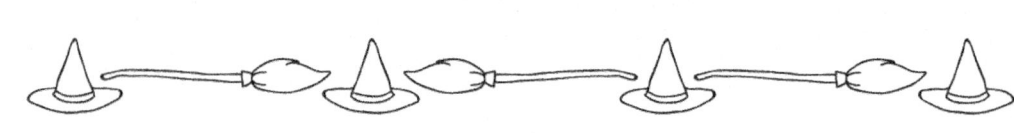

Would You Rather....

EAT A RAW CLOVE OF GARLIC **OR** EAT A RAW ONION?

Would You Rather....

Decorate your room with bats

OR

Decorate your room with skeletons?

Would You Rather....

Dress up as a devil **OR**  Dress up as a clown?

Would You Rather....

Own a pet rat

OR

Own a pet toad

WOULD YOU RATHER....

MAKE A SCARECROW

OR

COLLECT APPLES & MAKE APPLE JUICE?

WOULD YOU RATHER....

KISS A FROG   OR   KISS A SPIDER?

WOULD YOU RATHER....

IT WAS HALLOWEEN

OR

IT WAS CHRISTMAS?

WOULD YOU RATHER....

REMOVE A SPIDER FROM THE HOUSE **OR** RESCUE A CAT FROM A TREE?

Would You Rather....

live in a cave full of bats

OR

live in a house full of rats?

WOULD YOU RATHER...

BUILD A MONSTER
OR
WRAP UP A MUMMY?

Would You Rather....

Ride the night sky with a witch on her broomstick

OR

Walk the streets at night with a zombie?

WOULD YOU RATHER...

BLACK

OR

ORANGE?

WOULD YOU RATHER.....

Hold a Hallween party
or
Hold a scary movie night in?

WOULD YOU RATHER....

FIND OUT YOU'RE COSTUME IS IDENTICAL TO EVERYONE ELSE'S

OR

FIND OUT NO-ONE UNDERSTANDS WHAT YOUR COSTUME IS?

WOULD YOU RATHER....

Be enormous like a giant
or
Be small like a mouse?

WOULD YOU RATHER....

LOOK AFTER A 3 HEADED DOG

OR

LOOK AFTER A CRAZY DRAGON?

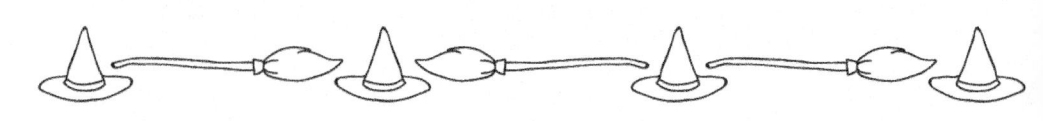

Would You Rather....

Have warts like a toad **OR** Have horns like a Monster?

Would You Rather....

Put your hand in a box of wriggling worms

OR Put your hand in a box of slimy slugs?

Would You Rather....

Eat a chocolate frog

OR

Eat popcorn?

Would You Rather....

Be chased by a vampire

OR

Be chased by a demon?

WOULD YOU RATHER....

Find a worm in your apple

OR

Find an eyeball in your ice cream

WOULD YOU RATHER....

SWIM IN SLIME

OR

STAND IN SOMETHING STICKY IN BARE FEET?

WOULD YOU RATHER....

Have a tube of fake blood

or

Have a tube of slime?

WOULD YOU RATHER....

HAVE ONE EYE IN THE MIDDLE OF YOUR HEAD **OR** HAVE TWO NOSES?

Would You Rather....

Walk on all fours like a cat

OR

Walk stiffly like a zombie?

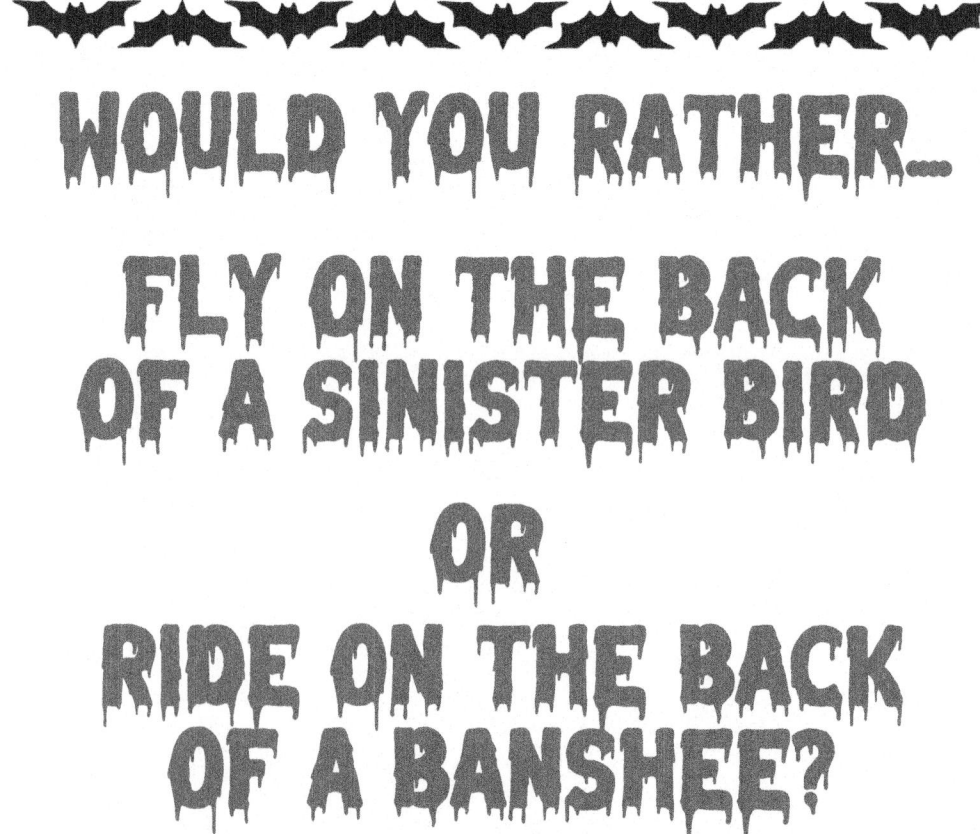

WOULD YOU RATHER...

FLY ON THE BACK OF A SINISTER BIRD

OR

RIDE ON THE BACK OF A BANSHEE?

Would You Rather....

Be able to cast spells like a witch

OR

Be able to predict the future?

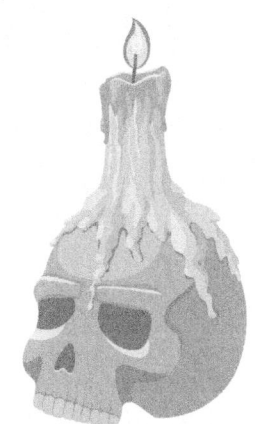

WOULD YOU RATHER...

SEE GHOSTS THAT NO-ONE ELSE CAN SEE

OR

NOT SEE GHOSTS THAT EVERYONE ELSE CAN SEE

WOULD YOU RATHER....

Be able to fly
or
Be invisible?

WOULD YOU RATHER....

NEVER HAVE TO WASH AGAIN

OR

NEVER HAVE TO CUT YOUR TOENAILS AGAIN

WOULD YOU RATHER....

Direct a scary movie

or

Write a ghost story?

WOULD YOU RATHER....

BE ABLE TO CONJURE UP RAIN AND STORMS

OR

BE ABLE TO MAGICALLY TALK TO ANIMALS?

Would You Rather....

Be able to float like a ghost **OR** Be able to walk through walls?

Would You Rather....

Go on a rollercoaster with a zombie

OR

Go sky diving with a wizard?

Would You Rather....

Wear a witch's hat all the time **OR** Have devil horns?

Would You Rather....

Have green hair like a witch

OR

Be furry all over like a werewolf?

WOULD YOU RATHER....

Drink sour milk

OR

Eat rotten eggs?

WOULD YOU RATHER....

CAST A SPELL TO TURN BACK TIME **OR** CAST A SPELL TO GIVE YOU UNLIMITED MONEY?

WOULD YOU RATHER....

WAIL LIKE A BANSHEE

OR

HOWL LIKE A WEREWOLF?

WOULD YOU RATHER....

BE TRAPPED IN A ROOM WITH A TALKING SKULL

OR

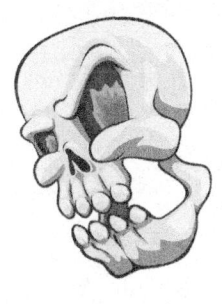

BE TRAPPED IN A ROOM WITH A SQUEAKING RAT?

Would You Rather....

Be able to jump and land like a cat OR

Be able to run fast sideways, like a spider?

WOULD YOU RATHER...
DECORATE FOR A HALLOWEEN PARTY
OR
CLEAR UP THE MESS AFTER A HALLOWEEN PARTY?

Would You Rather....

Eat a dead spider

OR

Eat a live worm?

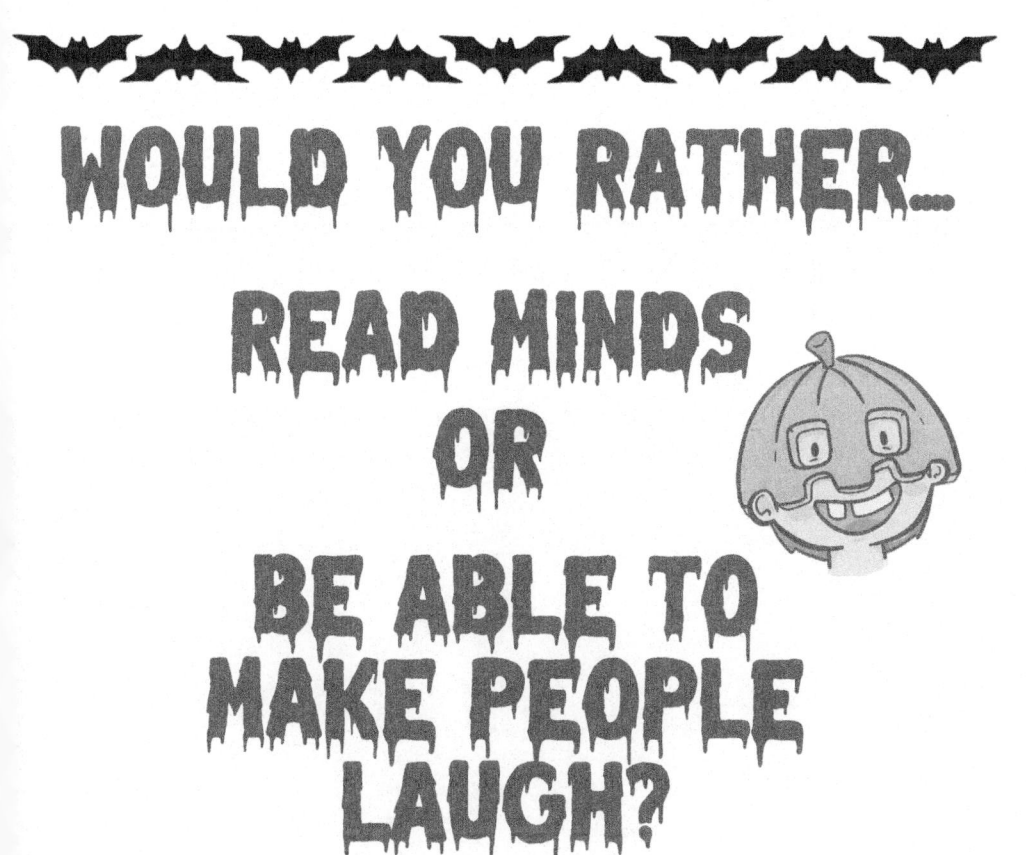

WOULD YOU RATHER...

READ MINDS
OR
BE ABLE TO MAKE PEOPLE LAUGH?

WOULD YOU RATHER.....

Own a love potion

or

Know a money spell?

WOULD YOU RATHER....

DISCOVER A SECRET DOOR

OR

A FRIEND TELLS YOU A SECRET?

WOULD YOU RATHER.....

A witch casts a spell to make you itchy
or
A witch casts a spell to make your friend itchy?

WOULD YOU RATHER....

TRY TO CATCH A FROG

OR

TRY TO CATCH A CAT?

Would You Rather....

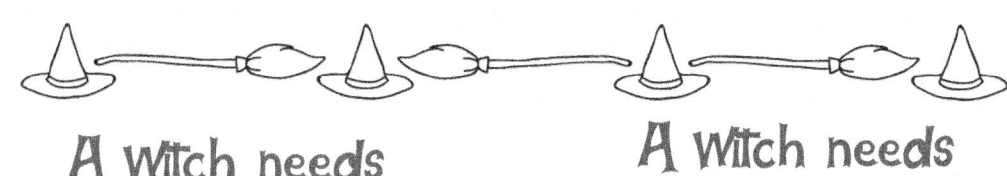

A witch needs one of your teeth for a spell

OR

A witch needs one of your toes for a spell

Would You Rather....

Wear a Halloween mask

OR Paint your face for Halloween?

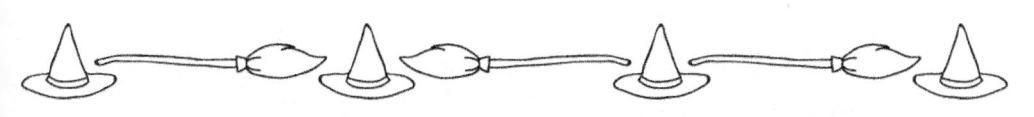

Would You Rather....

Brush a Werewolf's fur **OR** Give a Witch a Manicure?

Would You Rather....

Find out that your pumpkin got smashed **OR** Someone steals your trick or treat goodies?

WOULD YOU RATHER....

Wake up to find a creepy clown in your room **OR** Wake up to find a vampire in your room?

WOULD YOU RATHER....

HAVE A FRIEND WHO IS AN ALIEN **OR** HAVE A FRIEND WHO IS AN MONSTER

WOULD YOU RATHER....

Go Haunting as a ghost   OR

Dress in a scary costume and chase people?

WOULD YOU RATHER....

Design and make a haunted house   OR   Visit a haunted house someone else has made?

Would You Rather....

Get stuck in a bathroom with an angry rat

OR

Get stuck in a bathroom with an angry bat?

WOULD YOU RATHER...

SHARE A SLEEPING BAG WITH A NON VENOMOUS SNAKE

OR

SHARE A BED WITH A SKELETON

Would You Rather....

Be able to interpret dreams

OR

Be able to read people's minds?

WOULD YOU RATHER...

LEAD YOUR FAMILY INTO A HAUNTED HOUSE

OR

FOLLOW YOUR FAMILY INTO A HAUNTED HOUSE?

WOULD YOU RATHER.....

Eat buttered popcorn
or
Eat buttered sweetcorn?

WOULD YOU RATHER....

PLAY HALLOWEEN PARTY GAMES WITH FRIENDS
OR
GO OUT TRICK OR TREATING WITH FRIENDS

WOULD YOU RATHER.....

Hear a blood chilling scream

or

Hear the howl of a wild creature

WOULD YOU RATHER....

WALK ALONE THROUGH A DARK FOREST

OR

WALK ALONE THROUGH A DARK GRAVEYARD

Would You Rather....

See an apparition outside the window

OR

See a hissing black cat on the windowsill?

Would You Rather....

Find a pile of bones in a forest

OR

Meet a ghost who passes through you in the forest?

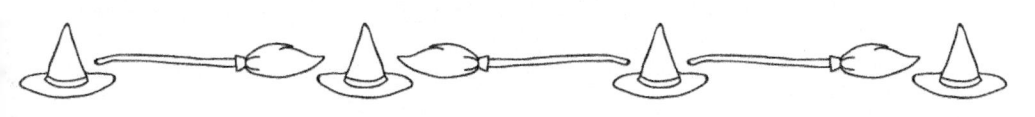

Would You Rather....

Own a Magic broomstick **OR** Own a Witches cauldron?

Would You Rather....

Your friend lets out a chilling cackle **OR** Your freind lets out a frightful howl?

WOULD YOU RATHER....

Your substitute teacher is a creepy clown

OR

Your substitute teacher is a scary demon

WOULD YOU RATHER....

LOOSE YOUR WAY IN FOG **OR** LOOSE YOUR WAY IN THE DARK?

WOULD YOU RATHER....

WALK THROUGH AN ENCHANTED FOREST

OR

VISIT A RUINED CASTLE?

WOULD YOU RATHER....

FEEL ICY COLD FINGERS ON YOUR ARM

OR

HEAR AN UNEXPLAINED BUMP IN THE NIGHT?

Would You Rather....

sleep in an isolated lighthouse

OR

sleep in an underground tunnel?

WOULD YOU RATHER...

YOUR FLASHLIGHT PICKS OUT A PAIR OF EYES

OR

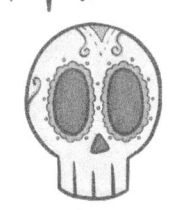

YOUR FLASHLIGHT PICKS OUT A PAIR OF FANGS

Would You Rather....

A goblin helps you with your schoolwork

OR

A genie grants you 3 wishes?

WOULD YOU RATHER...

IGNORE THE SHADOWS CAST BY CANDLELIGHT

OR

CHECK OUT THE ENTIRE ROOM BEFORE RELAXING?

You're a ghost:
WOULD YOU RATHER.....

Haunt someone you know
or
Haunt a stranger?

WOULD YOU RATHER....

FIGHT A NINJA

OR

FIGHT A WEREWOLF?

WOULD YOU RATHER....

It's a calm moonlit night
or
It's a wild and stormy night?

WOULD YOU RATHER....

KEEP A SKULL IN YOUR BEDROOM

OR

KEEP A LIVE SPIDER IN YOUR BEDROOM?

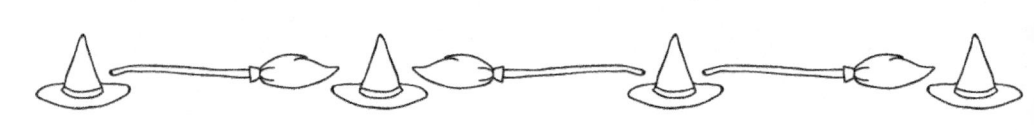

Would You Rather....

Go into a tomb with a friend **OR** Go into a tomb on your own?

Would You Rather....

You knew a spell to make other people vanish

OR

You knew a spell to make yourself vanish

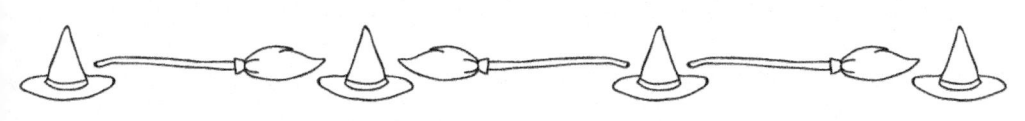

Would You Rather....

Spend 5 Minutes walking slowly across a ceMetary

OR

Spend 1 Minute lying in a grave?

Would You Rather....

Get a scary doll as a gift

OR

Give a scary doll as a gift?

WOULD YOU RATHER....

A WITCH CASTS A SPELL TO TURN YOU INTO A FROG

OR

A WITCH CASTS A SPELL TO TURN YOU INTO A STATUE

WOULD YOU RATHER....

HAVE DIRTY NAILS LIKE A WITCH

OR

HAVE A LAUGH THAT CACKLES LIKE A WITCH

WOULD YOU RATHER....

WRITE A BOOK OF SPELLS

OR

WRITE A BEST SELLING GHOST STORY?

WOULD YOU RATHER....

HIDE FROM A WEREWOLF IN A HOLLOW TREE **OR** HIDE FROM A GHOST UNDER YOUR BED?

Would You Rather....

A wizard makes your feet twice their normal size

OR

A wizard makes your hands twice their normal size?

WOULD YOU RATHER...

FLY ON A WITCH'S BROOMSTICK

OR

STIR A WITCH'S BUBBLING CAULDRON?

Would You Rather....

Be a witch's cat for one day

OR

Be a wizard's owl for one day?

WOULD YOU RATHER...

BE CHILLED TO THE BONE BY A GHOST

OR

BE HEATED UP TO BOILING BY A DEVIL?

WOULD YOU RATHER.....

Crawl through a dark tunnel

or

Run through a zombie crowd?

WOULD YOU RATHER....

SQUISH AN EYEBALL WITH YOUR FINGERS

OR

PUT YOUR HAND INTO A TUB OF MAGGOTS?

WOULD YOU RATHER....

Be chased by one fast zombie
or
Be chased by 10 slow zombies?

WOULD YOU RATHER....

WEAR A HALLOWEEN COSTUME MADE BY A 5 YEAR OLD

OR

WEAR A HALLOWEEN COSTUME YOU BOUGHT 5 YEARS AGO?

Would You Rather....

Run through a pit of rats to get to a Halloween party

OR

Crawl through a long, dark tunnel to get to a Halloween party

Would You Rather....

Own a magical giant owl you can ride on and fly

OR

Own a magical giant cat you can take for walks on a rope?

Would You Rather....

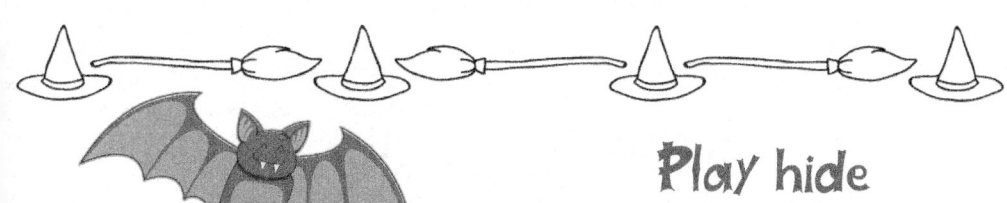

Play hide and seek in a cave full of bats **OR** Play hide and seek in a castle full of ghosts?

Would You Rather....

Catch a mouse to feed to a pet owl **OR** Catch 5 beetles to feed to a bat?

WOULD YOU RATHER....

Drink a witch's potion that makes you run 3 times faster

OR

Drink a witch's potion that makes you 3 times stronger?

WOULD YOU RATHER....

Compose a best-selling Halloween song that wins an award

OR

Discover proof of that the Sasquatch exists

WOULD YOU RATHER....

HAVE TO EAT YOUR BREAKFAST WITH A HARMLESS SNAKE IN THE KITCHEN

OR HAVE TO EAT YOUR BREAKFAST IN A PITCH DARK SHED?

WOULD YOU RATHER....

SPEND THE DAY WEARING A ZOMBIE COSTUME **OR** SPEND THE DAY WEARING A BAT COSTUME

Would You Rather....

A wizard grants you a wish to be able to control the weather

OR

A wizard grants you a wish to be able to control your teacher

WOULD YOU RATHER...

WATCH A SCARY MOVIE IN SLOW MOTION

OR

WATCH A SPOOKY MOVIE AT DOUBLE SPEED?

Would You Rather....

You can talk to animals

OR

You can talk in any language?

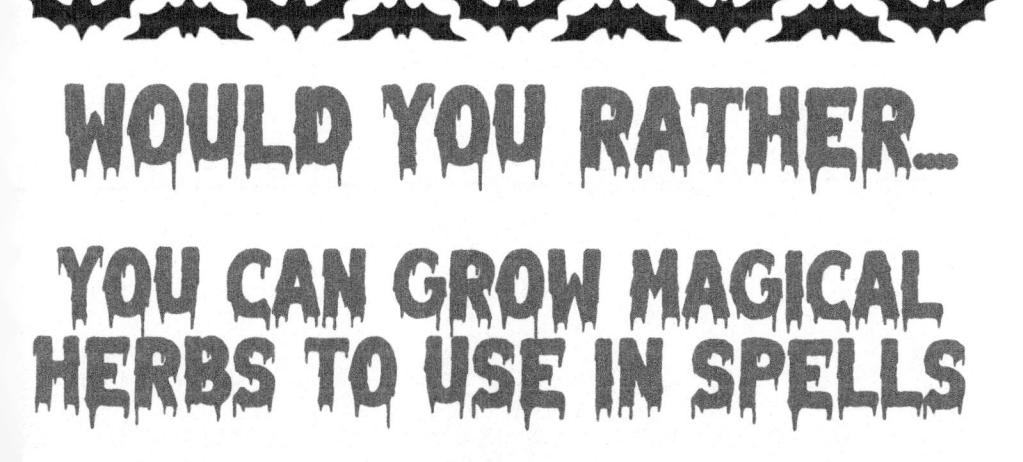

WOULD YOU RATHER...

YOU CAN GROW MAGICAL HERBS TO USE IN SPELLS

OR

YOU GROW THE BIGGEST PUMPKIN EVER SEEN?

WOULD YOU RATHER....

Go bowling with a skull
or
Play hockey with a broomstick?

WOULD YOU RATHER....

SAY 'CREEPY CRAWLER CRITTERS CRAWL THROUGH CREEPY CRAWLY CRATERS' 10 TIMES BEFORE BREAKFAST

OR

SAY 'IF TWO WITCHES WOULD WATCH TWO WATCHES, WHICH WITCH WOULD WATCH WHICH WATCH' 10 TIMES BEFORE DINNER

WOULD YOU RATHER....

Wear shoes with slimy soles that make you slip

or

Wear shoes with sticky soles that make you stick

WOULD YOU RATHER....

GO TO A HALLOWEEN PARTY WHERE EVERYONE SINGS LOUDLY INSTEAD OF SPEAKING

OR

GO TO A HALLOWEEN PARTY WHERE NO-ONE TALKS AT ALL

Would You Rather....

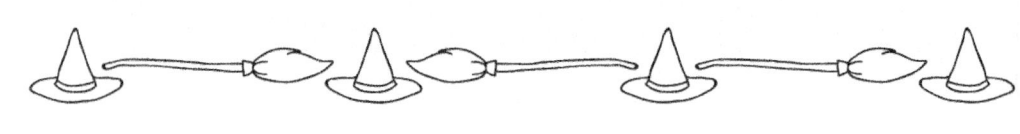

Eat a raw clove of garlic to ward off vampires

OR

Carry a stake of wood everywhere you go

Would You Rather....

Own an owl that can deliver trick or treat candy to your friends

OR

Own an owl that can perform a flying display for your friends?

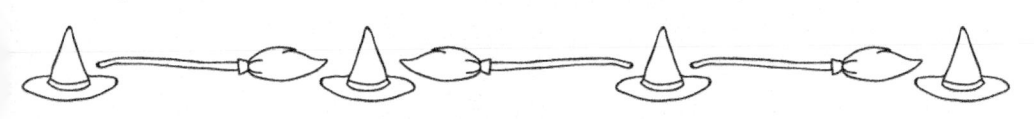

Would You Rather....

A witch casts a spell and you can't speak

OR

A witch casts a spell and you can't hear

Would You Rather....

Your Halloween costume has to be worn forever

OR

You have to go trick or treating with no Halloween costume?

WOULD YOU RATHER....

A wizard gives you a magic key that can open any door

OR A wizard gives you a potion that can cure any illness?

WOULD YOU RATHER....

Live in a beautiful enchanted castle you can never leave

OR

Live in an dirty dungeon but you can leave when you want

WOULD YOU RATHER....

Be given supernatural powers to see your own future

OR Be given supernatural powers to see other people's future

WOULD YOU RATHER....

Be bewitched so that music always makes you dance

OR

Be bewitched so that music always makes you sing along

Would You Rather....

stay young forever   OR own a fountain of youth that you can let people drink from so that they can stay young forever?

WOULD YOU RATHER...

BE ATTACKED BY A WITCH'S CAT

OR

BE ATTACKED BY A VAMPIRE'S BAT?

Would You Rather....

Be able to conjure up a storm
OR
Be able to conjure up sunshine?

WOULD YOU RATHER...

EAT A BRAIN SANDWICH

OR

EAT A ROCK OYSTER (BULL'S TESTICLE)?

WOULD YOU RATHER....

Be a vampire and bite people
or
Be a doctor and heal vampire bites?

WOULD YOU RATHER....

BE ABLE TO TELEPORT ANYWHERE

OR

BE ABLE TO READ PEOPLE'S MINDS

WOULD YOU RATHER....

Have a big wart on your nose like a witch

or

Have a thick fur on the back of your hands like a werewolf?

WOULD YOU RATHER....

BE FAMOUS FOR BEING BAD

LIKE DRACULA

OR

BE A NORMAL PERSON

WHOM EVERYONE LIKES?

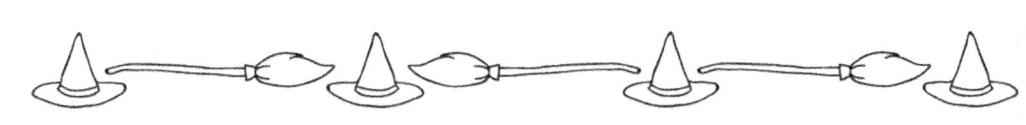

Would You Rather....

Find a Mummy's treasure trove but be cursed **OR** stick with what you have and not be cursed?

Would You Rather....

Be lost in a dark forest **OR** Be lost in a sketchy part of town?

Would You Rather....

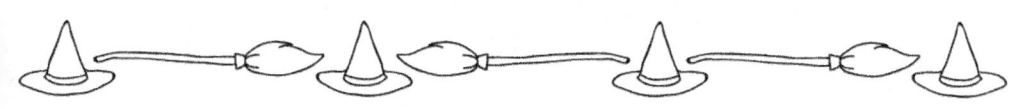

Be someeone who dissolves in water like a witch so you never can wash or go swimming

OR

Be someeone who dissolves in sunlight like a vampire so you cn't go outside unless it is dark?

Would You Rather....

Gather the ingredients for a witch's spell

OR

Make a witch's spell following a recipe?

WOULD YOU RATHER....

Go to a theme park on your own that has been themed for Halloween

OR

Go to a Halloween party with all your friends?

WOULD YOU RATHER....

CAST A BAD SPELL **OR** CAST A GOOD SPELL?

WOULD YOU RATHER....

INVENT AN AMAZINGLY DELICIOUS PUMPKIN DISH **OR** INVENT THE BEST EVER APPLE DISH?

WOULD YOU RATHER....

A CURSE GAVE YOU AN EXTRA BELLY BUTTON **OR** A CURSE GAVE YOU AN EXTRA EAR?

Would You Rather....

Have the power to open any door using just your mind

OR

Have the power to close any door using just your mind?

WOULD YOU RATHER...
HAVE THE POWER TO FOLLOW PEOPLE WITHOUT BEING NOTICED
OR
HAVE THE POWER TO WATCH PEOPLE WITHOUT BEING NOTICED

Would You Rather....

own a map that shows where all your friends are at any time

OR

own a map that shows where all the burried treasure lies

WOULD YOU RATHER...

BE FOLLOWED BY AN EVIL CLOWN

OR

BE FOLLOWED BY A DANGEROUS MUMMY?

WOULD YOU RATHER.....

Be trapped in a room with 50 spiders　　or　　Eat 10 spiders in 10 minutes

---

WOULD YOU RATHER....

AN EVIL SPELL MAKES ALL YOUR TEETH FALL OUT

OR

AN EVIL SPELL MAKES ALL YOUR HAIR FALL OUT?

WOULD YOU RATHER....

All your clothes are orange
or
All your clothes are black

WOULD YOU RATHER....

LIVE IN A WITCHES COVEN

OR

LIVE THROUGH A ZOMBIE APOCALYPSE?

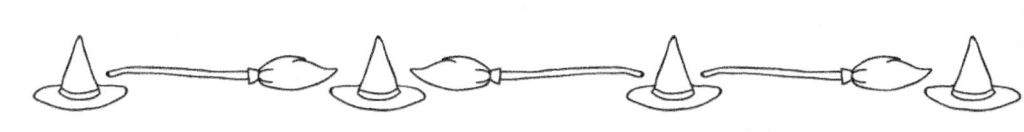

Would You Rather....

A rat licks your bare foot **OR** You have to lick a rats foot?

Would You Rather....

Be able to have complete control over fire

OR Be able to have complete control over water

Would You Rather....

A witch wants your toenail clippings for a spell **OR** You have to get a witch's toenail clippings for a spell

Would You Rather....

A witch shrinks all your clothes so they are slightly too small

OR A witch enlarges all your clothes so they are way too big?

WOULD YOU RATHER....

You could look into a mirror and re-live past events

OR You could look into a mirror and see your future self?

WOULD YOU RATHER....

BE BANDAGED FOR A WEEK LIKE A MUMMY **OR** HAVE GREEN HAIR FOR A WEEK LIKE A WITCH?